DISCOVER
Your Career

Careers If You Like **Working with Your Hands**

Stuart A. Kallen

ReferencePoint Press

San Diego, CA

ReferencePoint Press®

Printed in the United States

For more information, contact:
ReferencePoint Press, Inc.
PO Box 27779
San Diego, CA 92198
www.ReferencePointPress.com

LIBRARY OF CONGRESS CATALOGING-IN-PUBLICATION DATA

Names: Kallen, Stuart A., 1955– author
Title: Careers If You Like Working with Your Hands / by Stuart A. Kallen.
Description: San Diego, CA : ReferencePoint Press, Inc, 2026. | Series:
Discover Your Career| Includes bibliographical
references and index. |
Identifiers: LCCN 2025040491 (print)
9781678212261 lib. bdg. | ISBN 9781678212278 ebook
Subjects: LCSH: Juvenile literature | Vocational guidance

For compete cataloging-in-publication data please go to www.loc.gov.

Contents

Introduction: Skilled Workers in Demand

The rapid growth of artificial intelligence (AI) is creating a building binge in the United States. The world's biggest tech companies—including Amazon, Google, Microsoft, and Meta—are spending billions to construct specialized AI data centers. These massive buildings house servers, storage units, network devices, and other equipment used to process AI data. The high-tech machines generate a lot of heat, which means data centers rely on cooling systems called chillers. Each chiller requires four technicians trained to maintain heating, ventilating, and air-conditioning (HVAC) equipment. And there are not enough HVAC workers to meet the demand, according to David Gitlin, chief executive officer of Carrier Global, which produces chillers and other heating and cooling equipment. "We have 425,000 technicians today," says Gitlin, discussing the entire HVAC industry. "We are going to need to hire another four to five hundred thousand over the next 10 years."[1]

The AI data industry is only one sector in which demand for skilled laborers outstrips the supply. Other industries, including construction and manufacturing, are also growing rapidly while facing a shortage of qualified tradespeople. According to a 2024 report by the management consulting firm McKinsey & Company, new infrastructure and building projects are expected to create 345,000 skilled trade jobs by 2028. Analysts say an additional half a million jobs will be generated by the manufacturing sector. With high industry demand for trade and manufacturing laborers, those who like to work with their hands can expect to earn good wages in the coming years.

Better Prospects

A 2025 survey by Resume Builder found that 42 percent of workers born during the late 1990s to the early 2010s were employed in skilled trade jobs. Many were college graduates. Around one-third of these workers said their jobs offered them better long-term prospects. Resume Builder's chief career advisor, Stacie Haller, explains the findings: "More Gen Z college graduates are turning to trade careers and for good reason. Many are concerned about AI replacing traditional white-collar roles, while trade jobs offer hands-on work that's difficult to automate. Additionally, many grads find their degrees don't lead to careers in their field, prompting them to explore more practical, in-demand alternatives."[2]

Some who pursue more practical alternatives understand that they do not need expensive college degrees. A two-year associate's degree from a community college or technical school is all that is necessary to build an interesting career that combines manual proficiency with creative talent.

Rewarding Work

New workers in construction industry jobs earn while they learn. Apprentices in the building trades receive around 2,000 hours of paid on-the-job training while also taking 720 hours of classes at a technical school. (Each state has specific requirements for work hours and classroom hours.) After completing their apprenticeships, trade workers are qualified to work as independent contractors. And those who work with their hands in the construction industry have some of the highest levels of job satisfaction. A three-year survey of fifty-seven thousand workers by BambooHR found that construction was the "happiest" industry. Ninety percent of workers surveyed said they were satisfied with their jobs because their work offered meaning and value. Most said they would not enjoy working for a big corporation, and only 11 percent feared losing their jobs to AI. As Haller states:

> [These] jobs offer a smart and rewarding path for many, especially those who prefer hands-on work and practical

learning over traditional classroom settings. They provide faster entry into the workforce, often without the burden of student debt. . . . These jobs . . . can lead to career growth through specialization, supervisory roles, or even business ownership, making trades a viable and stable long-term career option.[3]

Not all hands-on jobs are in the construction industry. A wide range of jobs offer similar satisfaction. Those who work as artisans, fashion designers, cosmetologists, and bakers and chefs combine their manual proficiency with their creative instincts. Some—including physical therapists, dental hygienists, and sign language interpreters—work with their hands to improve the lives of others. And some jobs, like robotics technician and electronic engineering technologist, require workers to possess both traditional mechanical skills and expertise in cutting edge technology.

In 2025 the home maintenance technology company Thumbtack compiled a report about the future of skilled trades. The report found that 83 percent of young adult respondents said that "learning a skilled trade is sometimes a better pathway to economic security than going to college."[4] A similar number agreed that young people are often wrongly told that attending college is the best way to secure their future. But as chief executive officer of Thumbtack Marco Zappacosta says, "There's never been a better time to enter the trades, and as a generation shaped by the . . . gig economy, Gen Z are uniquely suited to a profession that offers flexibility and independence. With [an] . . . incredible demand for people to fill these roles, expertise in the trades is a future-proof career."[5]

Tattoo Artist

What Does a Tattoo Artist Do?

Some artists work with clay. Others work with paint and canvas. Tattoo artists express their creative talents by applying ink to arms, legs, and other body parts. And some tattoo artists like Nikko Hurtado earn millions and attract worldwide fame for their skills. Hurtado is famous for producing hyperrealistic tattoos that look like photos printed on skin. His work can be seen on celebrities such as movie star Dwayne "the Rock" Johnson and rappers Drake and Wale. Hurtado has over 2 million followers on Instagram and has appeared as a judge on the tattoo reality competition show *Ink Master.* He regularly receives high praise for his talents, but he attributes his success to his work ethic. "I just try to do my very best and I just try to add value to the things that I do," Hurtado says. "Like if I tattoo you, I try to do my very best and hopefully the value is when you show your tattoo, you'll feel proud of it."[6]

At a Glance

Number of Jobs
6,400 in 2025

Pay
$59,984 in 2025

Educational Requirements
None, but art classes are helpful

Personal Qualities
Artistic talent, steady hand, business and marketing acumen, people skills

Working Conditions
Full time, weekends, holidays, and late-night hours with overtime

Future Job Outlook
Growth of 3 percent through 2033*

* For all craft and fine artists

Tattoo artists always need to do their very best because tattoos are permanent. They are created by an artist using a tattoo machine. The machine has a rapidly pulsating needle that injects ink into the dermis layer of skin (below the outer layer of skin).

All tattoos start with artwork. Many tattoo artists create their own designs, and they also draw up unique designs based on the wishes of clients. Some tattoo artists primarily create sketches on paper, while other use computer software like Adobe Illustrator or tattoo-specific programs such as Tattoodo and Vagaro.

Before any ink is applied to skin, a tattoo artist explains the process to the client. Discussions include the amount of pain involved in creating the tattoo, the cost, and the length of time it will take to finish the skin art. Tattoo artists need to be sensitive to the needs of the client because tattoos are extremely personal. A customer might want a tattoo that honors a romantic partner or reminds them of a deceased friend, relative, or role model. The tattoo artist offers helpful suggestions as to the placement of the tattoo, since some parts of the body are more sensitive than others.

Most tattoo artists work with stencils. These are hand-drawn or digital designs that are printed out on transfer paper. The artist temporarily applies the stencil to the client's skin and uses it as a road map that shows where to place lines, shading, and colors.

One of the most important aspects of the tattoo artist's job is maintaining a safe and hygienic environment. People bleed when skin is pierced by tattoo needles. This increases the risk of infection and might also spread blood-borne diseases such as hepatitis and human immunodeficiency virus. A tattoo artist needs to ensure that the workstation, tattoo machine, and all other equipment are clean and sterilized. Artists must wash their hands with antibacterial soap before starting any procedure and wear disposable gloves when working on clients. Supplies like needles, ink capsules, razors, paper towels, and related items have to be properly disposed of after work is completed. Tattoo machines and other reusable equipment must be properly stored in sterile containers.

Develop Your Artistic Talents

"Tattooing is an art form and if you want to get into it and be good at it, then you need to be good at art. Spend your time learning the fundamentals of art. Go on YouTube and learn from guys like Stan Prokopenko and Marco Bucci. The skills you can learn from these artists online, will directly translate into tattooing. . . . [A good mentor] will respect you and your time and make sure you get educated in this industry the right way. Above all, never lose your drive for art. If you love doing art, then you will have the greatest time in this industry."

—Rusty Thornhill, tattoo artist

Quoted in Skin Artists, "Interview with Rusty Thornhill," March 11, 2022. www.skin-artists.com.

After tattoos are completed, the artist's work is not done. Aftercare procedures include wrapping the tattoo in plastic for an hour or two until bleeding stops. Tattoo artist Noemi Barajas explains how she counsels her clients when tattoo work is finished: "Definitely stay out of steam rooms, saunas, lakes—anywhere you could catch bacteria. If you go to the gym, don't have your skin exposed where you can, you know, put your arm up against a sweaty, like, gym equipment. . . . Because you can get an infection like that."[7]

A Typical Workday

Artistic talent is central to a tattoo artist's success, but their workday involves much more than tattooing skin. They must spend time attending to finances, marketing, training apprentice tattoo artists, and running a studio that will attract customers.

People do not generally get tattoos early in the day. Most tattoo studios open at noon and do not close until midnight or even later. If there are no client appointments in the afternoon, the tattoo artist does prep work while waiting for walk-in customers.

Tattoo artists express their creative talents by applying ink to arms, legs, and other body parts. Their primary tool is a rapidly pulsating needle that injects ink into the dermis layer of skin.

Preparations involve drawing new designs and working on specific designs for clients.

Tattoo artists spend time cleaning workspaces and ensuring that equipment is sterilized. Time is also dedicated to promoting their talents on social media. Tattoo artist Veronique Wiebe believes this aspect of the job is very important. She explains, "The internet is an endless world of marketing info—the tattoo artists of today need to pay attention to that part of their business—keep it simple to start, then develop further."[8]

Tattoo artists who own their own studio spend time managing the business, overseeing other artists, and instructing apprentices. Phone calls, emails, texts, and social media messages need to be answered. Consultations with prospective clients might be conducted with video calls or in person.

When customers come to receive tattoos, the artist carefully draws designs on the skin, using a wide variety of colored ink.

Small tattoos can be completed in a few minutes, while others require hours of meticulous work.

Education and Training

Hurtado says he fell in love with art as a young boy and began drawing as soon as he could hold a pencil. He decided to pursue a career as a tattoo artist when he was fifteen, three years before he could legally get a tattoo. Hurtado says that when he finally got his first tattoos, he was motivated by a desire to learn: "I got my forearms tattooed in order to watch my heroes [at work] and deconstruct what they were doing and then take it back and do what they were doing."[9]

Hurtado's path is similar to that of most tattoo artists. They start their careers learning from others in the trade. Some also take art courses in high school or study art in college. Whatever their educational background, prospective tattoo artists must have a good portfolio of their best artwork to land an apprenticeship. A portfolio is like an artistic résumé that exhibits an artist's creativity, style, and talent. Graphic designers and other visual artists—including tattoo artists—generally post their portfolios on a personal website so that prospective employers and clients can freely examine them.

In the United States individuals need to be at least eighteen years old to become apprentice tattoo artists. Regulations vary in different states and counties, but in some places tattoo artists must have a license to practice. They might need to complete online courses from state or local health departments that cover issues like hygiene, first aid, and protecting against blood-borne diseases.

Skills and Personality

Most tattoo artists are drawn to their work because they are dedicated to art and design. They spend countless hours practicing

Placing the Tattoo on the Body

"I always print out my designs . . . a large, a medium and a small. And then I cut [each] out, and I have [the client] go stand in front of the mirror and [I] say . . . put [each one] on your body and kind of play around with it and look at where you'd want it, you know, because that's kind of, like, what it's going to look like. So if you want to go small—you don't want to make a huge statement, then go with a small one. If you want to . . . really show it off . . , go big or go home, you know."

—Noemi Barajas, tattoo artist

Quoted in Lilianna Maria Percy Ruiz, "Thinking of Getting Inked? Start with a Tiny Tattoo," NPR, February 15, 2024. www.npr.org.

their drawing, which helps them develop a steady hand and a keen eye. Many try to avoid drugs and alcohol because this can affect their work. Even coffee can cause the hand to shake slightly, which can create problems for a tattoo artist. In addition to being artists, they need to excel at business, marketing, and customer relations.

Workplace Settings

Tattoo artists usually work in storefront shops, sometimes referred to as tattoo studios or tattoo parlors. Applying permanent ink to skin is demanding both mentally and physically. The tattoo artist can experience stress when striving to create a perfect masterpiece, ever aware that a slight slip of the hand can create a permanent problem for the client. Tattoo artists spend hours hunching over their work, and that can lead to back, neck, and eye strain. Tattoo machines vibrate constantly, which can cause nerve or muscle problems with wrists and hands.

Employers and Pay

Most tattoo artists charge by the hour for their services. Prices vary depending on the location and the previous experience of the artist. In 2024 tattoo artists were earning an average of $150 an hour, according to the Tattooing 101 website. Around 40 percent of this rate goes back into the business to pay for ink, needle cartridges, surgical gloves, shop rental, utilities, bookkeeping services, and other necessities. After deducting expenses, the average salary for a tattoo artist in 2025 was $59,984, according to the employment website Indeed. However, tattoo artists with the best reputations and celebrity clients can earn much more, and those with the most expertise bring in over $300,000 annually.

What Is the Future Outlook for Tattoo Artists?

The Bureau of Labor Statistics does not track employment growth for tattoo artists but predicts that the number of jobs for all craft and fine artists will grow by 3 percent through 2033, which is slightly less than the average growth rate of 4 percent for all professions. However, in 2025 around one-third of all Americans had at least one tattoo, and the popularity of skin art continues to grow. According to Fortune Business Insights, the global tattoo market is expected to double in value to $4.8 billion from 2025 to 2030. And the tattoo market in the United States is expected reach a value of $1.25 billion by 2032. These figures show that the demand for tattoo artists will likely rise faster than the demand for other artists as more people choose to decorate their body with skin art.

Find Out More

Alliance of Professional Tattooists (APT)
https://safe-tattoos.com
The APT advocates for tattoo artists and the tattoo trade. Its website offers seminars and comprehensive information about health and safety measures, the history of skin art, and educational resources.

Global Tattoo Association
www.global-tattoo.com
This association caters to tattoo apprentices and professional artists. Visitors to its website can find blogs, training and employment information, business guides, and news about tattoo festivals.

Tattooing 101
https://tattooing101.com
Tattooing 101 is an online tattoo school. Its website offers courses and features blogs, student stories, forums, and other information useful to prospective tattoo artists.

Electrician

What Does an Electrician Do?

Carl Murawski wanted a job in the construction trade that relied more on brains than brawn. He hoped to use his problem-solving skills on the job rather than performing manual labor, like swinging a hammer or carrying heavy bricks. This led Murawski to become an electrician. Electricians read blueprints and wiring diagrams, and they have a strong knowledge of voltages, circuitry, and power sources. They install wiring, electrical outlets, light fixtures, electronics for solar array and battery systems, lines for appliances, and components such as fuse boxes and transformers. Those who work as electricians use various measuring tools to check and troubleshoot systems, including ammeters, voltmeters, thermal scanners, and cable testers. They work with screwdrivers, wire strippers, and power tools. Murawski says being an electrician offers more variety than other jobs in the skilled trades: "I've found myself working alongside a railroad track in the middle of a state forest, inside a nuclear submarine base, and keeping my lunch away from snapping turtles in a swamp."[10]

At a Glance

Number of Jobs
779,800 in 2024

Pay
$62,350 in 2024

Educational Requirements
High school diploma, apprenticeship

Personal Qualities
Color vision, critical-thinking skills, physical strength and stamina, good communication skills, math skills

Working Conditions
Full time in homes, at businesses, and on construction sites; chance of electric shocks

Future Job Outlook
Growth of 11 percent through 2033

Without electricians there would be no safe, reliable sources of electricity for the lights and appliances that power modern civilization. Most electricians are union members, classified as journeymen by the International Brotherhood of Electrical Workers (IBEW). Experienced electricians often work as specialists. Residential or house electricians can be found wiring new buildings at home construction sites. They also make house calls when customers need repair or installation services. Electricians referred to as inside wiremen or wireworkers perform similar tasks in larger structures such as office buildings, airports, schools, government buildings, and arenas. Those who work in factories install and repair electric motors and machinery.

Telecommunications electricians lay fiberoptic cables and install systems used for telephones, intercoms, computer networks, and security and fire alarms. Those known as linemen or line workers spend their days outdoors, installing and repairing utility wires that run from power plants to local transformers, and then to homes and other buildings.

Electricians are required to follow local and state building regulations that are based on the National Electrical Code (NEC). The NEC, part of the National Fire Code published by the National Fire Protection Association, is a series of standards designed to ensure the safe installation of electrical wiring and equipment.

A Typical Workday

Workdays for electricians depend on their specialty. Those who install wiring in new structures spend their days on construction sites. They install conduit (plastic pipes that hold wires) in unfinished walls and floors. They feed wires through the conduit and hook up entire systems to light switches, wall outlets, and fuse boxes. Residential electricians who focus on maintenance and repairs have a more difficult job. Electrical problems often result from loose or exposed wires hidden in walls. These unprotected

Educate Yourself

"[You] will have to work hard and ask for not expect knowledge to be given to you. It very rarely does, regardless if that is your journey worker's [i.e., supervising mentor's] job to do. They might not teach you, they might consider it threatening to their position and they might also just find it troublesome. You need to show them that it would be neither of those things to just teach you what you came to learn. . . . Look up videos on YouTube, go bend some pipe, find out how and why transformers work, look up YouTube videos on a day in the life."

—Diligent_Height962, electrician

Quoted in Reddit, "What Is Day to Day Like as an Electrician?," 2024. www.reddit.com.

wires may cause fuses to blow, which shuts off power to all or part of a residence. Exposed wires can also cause sparks that start fires. To address these hazards, electricians investigate outlets and switches and even knock holes in walls to get to faulty wiring. Murawski, who works as a residential electrician on construction sites, says the job provides him with great satisfaction. "Completing an electrical installation is a clear example of seeing the results of your effort," he writes. "You start the day and there's nothing but a bare ceiling, by the time you leave, there is a whole rack of cascading conduit leading to a new panel. It's a real feeling of accomplishment."[11]

Like all electricians, Murawski takes safety precautions very seriously. Electricians can be shocked, burned, or electrocuted by open circuits called hot wires. When high-voltage electricity surges through a human body, the muscles clench and the victim cannot let go of the wire. As electrician Kwon Pan writes, "When I worked as an electrician's apprentice, I probably was presented 20 opportunities to get shocked every hour of my work day. . . .

[However, with all those] opportunities to get shocked, I have only been shocked 3 times."[12] Pan notes that most shocks are not fatal, but all electricians understand that strong jolts of electricity can kill a person in a matter of seconds.

Those who work with high-voltage electricity wear rubber insulating gloves, known as hot gloves or electrical gloves. These gloves can slow down work and become a hindrance when handling small wires and screws, but they are essential to protect electricians from surprise shocks.

Education and Training

Electricians use math every day. High school students hoping to become electricians can get a jump on their career by learning geometry and elementary algebra. Basic physics courses that focus on electromagnetism and other electrical phenomena are also helpful. These topics form the basis of electrician apprenticeship programs that are taught in technical schools. Classroom instruction focuses on electrical theory, math, blueprint reading, circuitry, electrical code requirements, communications and fire alarm systems, and safety and first-aid practices. Apprentices also participate in two thousand hours of paid, on-the-job training.

Building contractors and unions sponsor apprenticeship programs. Those who contact their local union can learn exactly what they need to do to become an apprentice.

Skills and Personality

Electricians work with electrical systems that might be brand-new or out-of-date. This requires electricians to have a good understanding of complex codes, equipment, and power control systems. They need good critical-thinking skills to perform tests, diagnose problems, and troubleshoot equipment. Good math skills are essential, and attention to detail is important since small errors can result in big problems.

An electrician installs wiring at a construction site. Electricians also install electrical outlets, light fixtures, electronics for solar array and battery systems, lines for appliances, and more.

The job requires physical strength and stamina because electricians need to be able to lift and carry at least 50 pounds (22.7 kg). Electricians are required to communicate clearly with apprentices and other workers and need to be friendly when addressing customers, vendors, and others. Color-blind people cannot become electricians because of the high risk of electrical shocks. Wires are identified by color, and hot wires are usually red, one of the problematic shades for many people with color blindness.

Workplace Settings

Electricians work indoors, whether at homes, businesses, or construction sites. They work full time and often spend their days in cramped spaces, bending, kneeling, and stretching while installing light fixtures, outlets, and wiring. A journeyman electrician posted on Reddit that prospective electricians should "expect

Great Job, Great Pay

"The compensation for work as an IBEW member is amazing, and you can't find it anywhere else. As apprentices, we get paid as we're learning the trade, and the benefits are tremendous. . . . I look forward to always having work, especially because in the union you can go anywhere and work anywhere—you'll never be out of work, even if you have to travel for it. . . . And I like doing the work—I love seeing things in progress. So I'm excited for the next 10 to 15 years doing this work where I am and who I'm with."

—Dalton Thompson, apprentice wireman

Dalton Thompson, "The Electrical Worker," IBEW, August 1, 2025. https://ibew.org.

rain, expect sun, expect no AC, expect mud, dirt, grime, oil, paint, fire caulk, PVC glue."[13]

Working with high-voltage power lines is dangerous, and line workers are outdoors in all types of weather. According to the Electrical Safety Foundation, 195 electricians died from exposure to electricity during 2011 to 2022, the latest year for which figures were available. While any death on the job is unfortunate, these fatalities make up only a small percentage out of a workforce of around 779,800. Electricians have a far higher chance of dying in an automobile accident on the way to work than while performing their duties.

Despite the few fatalities, almost all electricians experience minor shocks on the job. Most injuries, however, come from cuts and scrapes caused by sharp copper wires. Electricians are at risk of burns from welding equipment, exposure to fumes from lead solder, and contact with toxic chemicals. In older buildings, electricians can be exposed to hazardous asbestos insulation and mold. Other risks are shared by all construction workers. For instance, electricians may fall off ladders, trip over construction debris, and risk injury from lifting heavy equipment.

Line workers are on call at night and over weekends to respond to emergencies. They are often the first people on the road after extreme weather events like hurricanes, tornadoes, ice storms, and snowstorms, working to repair lines and bring electricity back to local residents.

Employers and Pay

Some electricians are self-employed. Others work for electrical or building contractors. Electricians are also employed by electrical utilities, telecommunications companies, manufacturers, and governments. According to the Bureau of Labor Statistics (BLS), the average annual wage for an electrician was $62,350 in 2024. Those who worked for government agencies earned an average of $71,820, while those who were employed by electrical contractors earned $62,290.

What Is the Future Outlook for Electricians?

Electricians will remain in demand as long as lights are burning and generators are turning. The BLS says general employment for electricians will grow 11 percent through 2033, much faster than the average 4 percent growth rate for all professions. Demand will be slightly higher in the alternative power industry. There, as the demand for alternative energy grows, more electricians will be required to install solar and wind generators, along with backup batteries and other equipment.

Find Out More

International Brotherhood of Electrical Workers (IBEW)

https://ibew.org

The website of the IBEW provides information about electrical work in numerous economic sectors, including construction, manufacturing, and telecommunications. Visitors to the website can learn about career and educational opportunities, scholarships, union membership, and apprentice positions.

National Electrical Contractors Association (NECA)
www.necanet.org
The NECA is a trade organization for the electrical construction industry that shares information about building codes, safety management, and union membership. Visitors to the website can find out about educational programs, including online training courses, webinars, and apprenticeships.

National Fire Protection Association (NFPA)
www.nfpa.org
The NFPA publishes the National Fire Code, a set of safety standards for installing electrical wiring and equipment. The association's website offers information on training and certification in various programs that focus on industrial hazards, fire protection, and electrical installation.

Archaeologist

What Does an Archaeologist Do?

Sarah W. Neusius is an archaeologist at the Carnegie Museum of Natural History in Pittsburgh. Neusius specializes in zooarchaeology, the study of animal remains at archaeological sites. Her work focuses on the relationship between animals and early humans. Neusius explains:

> For me, opening a bag of bone refuse from a site still is exciting. Bone identification work is a little like doing a jigsaw puzzle without all the pieces. It is challenging, and it takes concentration and careful observation to piece together what you can. There is so much to figure out about any single piece of bone! What animal is it? How healthy was the animal? What part of the animal's body is it? Has it been burned or cut? How was the bone buried and changed after the humans were done with it?[14]

At a Glance

Number of Jobs
8,700 in 2023*

Pay
$64,910 in 2024*

Educational Requirements
Master's degree

Personal Qualities
Good physical condition, critical-thinking skills, eye for detail, good communication skills

Working Conditions
Full time in offices and classrooms; long, irregular hours at excavation sites

Future Job Outlook
Growth of 8 percent through 2033*

* For anthropologists and archaeologists

Archaeologists in most fields view their work as puzzle solving. They use tools like shovels, pickaxes, trowels, brushes, and sifters to unearth bones, pottery shards, weapons, and other

Digging in the Dirt

"When you go on [an archaeological] dig, then you can expect to dig! Archaeology is, first and basically, manual labor. The idea is to remove dirt carefully enough that we can tell exactly how things came to be situated as they were, and to record it carefully enough that we can reconstruct what happened in the past. We dig carefully because we want to know the context of every find—that's actually the single most important piece of information we are after. Knowing the context of something can make all the difference in how we understand it."

—Andrea M. Berlin, archaeology professor, Boston University

Andrea M. Berlin, "A Career in Archaeology," Archaeological Institute of America, 2025. www.archaeological.org.

items at archaeological sites. These fragments of past cultures are meticulously measured, photographed, cataloged, and pieced together to create a bigger picture of societies that existed hundreds—or thousands—of years ago.

In addition to using time-tested digging techniques, some archaeologists employ high-tech tools in their work, like the terrain-mapping technology lidar. In 2024 archaeologists used lidar to locate the remains of a two-thousand-year-old city hidden beneath the thick tree canopy in the Amazon rainforest in Ecuador. Another example is DNA sequencing techniques, which have been used to find out more about the people who were killed when Mount Vesuvius erupted in Pompeii, Italy, in 79 CE. And artificial intelligence is revealing more figural shapes within the massive ancient earthworks in Peru known as the Nazca lines.

Like Neusius, most archaeologists are specialists. Prehistoric archaeologists focus on the artistic, social, agricultural, and spiritual components of ancient cultures that thrived before written records were compiled. Classical archaeologists mostly study ancient Greek and Roman societies. Historical archaeologists analyze ancient and more recent peoples who kept written and pictorial records. Underwater archaeologists dive into oceans, lakes, and rivers to excavate and analyze submerged settlements and sunken ships. Other archaeology specialists focus on distinct regions and historical eras, such as the medieval period in Europe.

A Typical Workday

Archaeological sites are referred to as digs for a reason, as archaeology professor Andrea M. Berlin emphasizes. "We break up dirt with pick-axes, shovel it into buckets, and haul it away with wheelbarrows," she says. "As soon as we find something, however, we turn to smaller tools, such as trowels, small picks, whisk brooms and dust pans, and even toothbrushes and dental picks. Often there is a back-and-forth: hard digging with larger tools followed by careful, slow cleaning."[15]

Archaeologists often wake up before the sun rises and arrive at digs early in the morning, sometimes by 5:00 a.m. Digging ends by early afternoon. This schedule allows archaeologists to avoid working during the hottest part of the day. After eating, resting, and showering, archaeologists spend the rest of the afternoon in tents or other shelters cleaning, studying, and cataloging their finds. They might return to a dig site later in the day to take photos and map out the architecture of the site using tape measures and digital gauges. Some work into the early evening reading about new discoveries, updating research papers, and communicating with colleagues.

A period of digging at a site is called a season, and a season can last anywhere from a few weeks to several months. Some projects go on for many seasons because sites can be very large. Digs can even continue over the course of centuries; the first excavation of the Roman ruins at Pompeii was in 1748, and work continues there today.

An archaeologist works at a dig site in Bulgaria, part of an effort to learn how people in that area lived in the ancient past. Archaeologists use a variety of tools for their work, including shovels, pickaxes, trowels, brushes, and sifters.

At extensive digs, archaeologists might work with teams that can be quite large. Collections assistant Sam Tabner says that as a student she worked with two hundred people excavating the ruins of an ancient Roman town near Silchester, England. The dig site, in the middle of a farmer's field, employed professional chefs to feed the large crew. Students were assigned various tasks, from excavating and recording items to cleaning the portable toilets. As Tabner writes:

> My favorite task was the hands-on excavation work. This is where you get to dig the ground to unearth amazing artefacts such as Roman brooches and rings . . . some of which have not been seen or touched in over 2,000 years! It's an amazing and proud moment when you dig up something deemed rare or spectacular by professional archaeologists, especially if it then becomes the "find of the day."[16]

Education and Training

Most archaeologists have either a master's degree or a PhD in archaeology or anthropology, a closely related field of study. Neusius says her path to becoming an archaeologist began in high school when she took an anthropology course. Anthropologists do not dig in the dirt. They study historical documents, religious texts, artwork, languages, and other cultural resources to draw conclusions about a particular society. During her anthropology studies, Neusius worked part time at the Logan Museum of Anthropology in Beloit, Wisconsin. She became fascinated by the various artifacts she cleaned and organized at the museum. This led her to pursue a career in archaeology.

Prospective archaeologists can follow Neusius's path while in high school and take courses that focus on anthropology, history, geography, math, science, and languages. And those who manage archaeological digs are always looking for high school student volunteers to fill summer internships.

College-level coursework in archaeology focuses on principles of archaeology and anthropology, laboratory methods of archaeology, and biological and zoological aspects of archaeology. Students also study ancient history, including origins of human societies, art and architecture, and religions. Some focus on specific areas of study such as ancient China or the Middle East. Berlin cautions, "You can't rush graduate school. . . . Graduate school has three main parts: three to four years of courses, a year of studying for and then taking exams, and finally, writing a dissertation, which is really a kind of book; this usually take another three to four years."[17]

Almost all archaeology students spend their summers excavating at digs. At some digs students are charged for room and board and sometimes tuition if college credit is available. However, there are numerous research grants and travel fellowships available to graduate students.

Skills and Personality

An archaeologist's work requires critical-thinking skills, persistence, and a highly developed eye for detail. They must be on the lookout for miniscule fragments of bone, pottery, and other objects that are hidden in the earth. To perform in the field, archaeologists should be in good physical condition. They need to be able to bend, climb, and wield pickaxes and shovels for long periods. This work can be extremely tedious. Communication skills are also important for archaeologists, who need to detail their findings in research papers and to colleagues, students, and general audiences.

Workplace Settings

Archaeologists work full time in offices, classrooms, labs, and museums. Those employed at digs might work long hours at irregular schedules that include nights and weekends. Most spend time traveling to remote excavation sites. An archaeologist who blogs under the name Smiti says she has worked in Hungry, Ethiopia, Oman, India, and France. Smiti writes, "This has allowed me to spend months (even years) in many places and understand what it means to live, study, work, and travel in different countries."[18]

Any archaeologist will admit that digs are dirty and dangerous. Archaeologists deal with sunburn, heatstroke, dehydration, and even frostbite in some cases. Animals like rattlesnakes and bears can intrude on dig sites, but archaeologists most commonly deal with stinging scorpions, biting mosquitos, and disease-spreading ticks. Archaeologists get blisters on their hands from digging and might be injured by unstable terrain or crumbling structures. Sometimes they are exposed to hazardous chemicals. Archaeologist Mara Kaktins writes, "Arsenic was a major embalming ingredient in the 19th century, and since

Recordkeeping Is Important

"Even though I love digging, I spend a lot more of my time holding a pen than a trowel or a brush. Whenever anyone is digging, we also have someone recording the finds, including where they were found and what they were found with. This information is called provenience. An artifact without provenience has a lot less value to archaeologists, because we can't use it to answer many of the questions we want to ask: how was it used? When was it in use? What other objects were in use by the same people or at the same time?"

—Kristin Hacken, archaeologist and author

Kristin Hacken, "4. Recording Finds," Kristin Hacken personal website, 2025. www.kristinhacken.com.

archaeologists are frequently called in to identify and remove burials, arsenic is a significant consideration. . . . Mercury was considered a type of cure and used to treat various ailments . . . and just like arsenic, it doesn't go away in the soil."[19]

Employers and Pay

Archaeologists find employment at museums, historic sites, and parks. Some teach at colleges and universities. According to the Society for American Archaeology, most archaeologists are employed by cultural resource management (CRM) companies. CRM firms ensure that federal historic preservation laws are followed during construction projects. In such cases archaeologists assess potential building sites and ensure that historical artifacts, if present, are removed or protected during construction.

The Bureau of Labor Statistics (BLS) places archaeologists and anthropologists in the same category. The average annual wage for these professionals was $64,910 in 2024.

What Is the Future Outlook for Archaeologists?

The BLS predicts that employment for archaeologists and anthropologists will grow by 8 percent through 2033, which is twice the average growth rate for all professions. Archaeology is considered a relatively new discipline, and interest in this science is expected to grow as archaeologists make new discoveries using the latest high-tech tools.

Find Out More

American Anthropological Association (AAA)

https://americananthro.org

This professional organization publishes more than twenty journals, offers career planning services, and supports college and university anthropology and archaeology departments. The AAA sponsors summer internships, awards prizes and fellowships, and provides K–12 educational resources.

Archaeological Institute of America (AIA)

www.archaeological.org

The AIA was founded in 1879 to advance archaeology education, awareness, and fieldwork. The institute offers interactive digs online, publishes *Archaeology* magazine, and provides lesson plans for students and educators.

Society for American Archaeology (SAA)

www.saa.org

The SAA is dedicated to researching, interpreting, and protecting the archaeological heritage of the Americas. The society's website provides career counseling, a jobs board, and information on student internships.

Prosthetist

What Does a Prosthetist Do?

Phil Stevens knows what it is like to be in the company of a person who is missing a limb: "My uncle lost his arm in a hang gliding accident in his young adult years," Stevens says. "Growing up, I have vivid memories of watching him button his shirts and eat cornflakes with his prosthesis."[20] A prosthesis, sometimes referred to as an appliance, is an artificial limb that replaces an arm, leg, or other body part. Prostheses are created from a combination of materials that might include silicone, rubber, plastic, carbon fiber, and metals such as titanium, stainless steel, and aluminum. Some prostheses incorporate battery-operated microprocessors and hydraulic systems that give users enhanced mobility and control.

Stevens's childhood experiences led him to become a prosthetist, a health care technician who makes artificial limbs and fits them to patients' bodies. He works in a field of medicine called prosthetics that focuses on prescribing, making, and managing artificial limbs. Prosthetics is closely related to another branch of medicine called orthotics. Professionals who specialize in

At a Glance

Number of Jobs
9,100 in 2023

Pay
$78,310 in 2024

Educational Requirements
Master's degree

Personal Qualities
Compassionate, good communication skills, detail oriented, dexterous

Working Conditions
Full time in clinics, hospitals, and laboratories; physical activities that include bending, crouching, and lifting

Future Job Outlook
Growth of 15 percent through 2033

orthotics are called orthotists. They do not make artificial limbs but create braces, splints, and other supports for injured spines, knees, wrists, and other existing body parts.

Some prosthetists are also trained orthotists, and the work is similar because they help patients recover mobility. Prosthetic technology has significantly advanced since the days of wooden legs and hand hooks. Micropowered ankles and knees mimic muscles and tendons in the leg and allow a user to walk with a natural gait while preventing stumbles and falls. Fingers in prosthetic hands incorporate tiny motors with microprocessors that allow for more than a dozen selectable grip patterns. Specialized devices can be made to grip a variety of items, including baseballs, golf clubs, work tools, and even musical instruments.

Patients can receive prosthetic feet specially designed for activities that include walking, running, and playing sports. Running blades are used by track and field athletes, while cyclists, swimmers, and skiers can obtain prostheses to pursue their own athletic goals.

A Typical Workday

On an average day, Stevens says he sees around ten patients. But he might spend an entire day and even work overtime with a single patient who has particularly complicated problems. "The goal is to work a traditional day," Stevens says. "But the fact is that the job isn't done until the individual is cared for."[21]

Prosthetists work closely with physicians to discuss details of each patient's injuries, medical conditions, and physical abilities. Individual patients are interviewed and examined to determine what types of prostheses would help them. Since every patient's needs are unique, a prosthetist will design and fabricate each prosthesis. First a precise mold of the remaining part of the limb is made with a plaster cast or 3-D scanning technology. The prosthetist then creates a blueprint for the limb using computer-aided

Working with a New Patient

"My [11:00 a.m.] appointment is a diagnostic fitting for a test socket. This patient is a new prosthesis user, so I educate him on how to put on the prosthesis. The patient is able to stand and start walking in the parallel bars. While he walks, I make adjustments to the alignment of the prosthesis to help achieve smooth gait mechanics. This is the first time he has walked since his amputation! I usually find that my patients are very excited for their first walking appointments. They say they feel like they are finally getting part of their lives back that they lost due to amputation."

—Jessica Smit, prosthetist

Jessica Smit, "A Day in the Life: Jessica Smit, Certified Prosthetist Orthotist," Shirley Ryan AbilityLab, April 23, 2025. www.sralab.org.

design and manufacturing software like AutoCAD, SolidWorks, and SketchUp. After the designs are completed, prosthetists have several options. Some collaborate with medical appliance technicians to fabricate the prothesis in their clinic's lab, sometimes with the aid of a 3-D printer. The designs might also be submitted to one of the many companies that manufacture custom prosthetics. Prosthetist Annie Crain says she uses her technical skills to fabricate prosthetic devices herself: "The fabrication process from start to finish of most devices typically includes: a cast of the affected area which is used to create a positive plaster model, modifying the positive model by sanding or carving the plaster to acquire the desired shape, then draping hot plastic or pouring resin over the positive model. The cooled plastic or resin lamination will then be cut and smoothed into a finished product."[22]

The next stage is fitting the device to the residual limb. The prosthetist ensures that the prosthesis fits, functions, and is comfortable to wear and use. Prosthetist offices have a variety of equipment that allows patients to test their appliances in a safe manner.

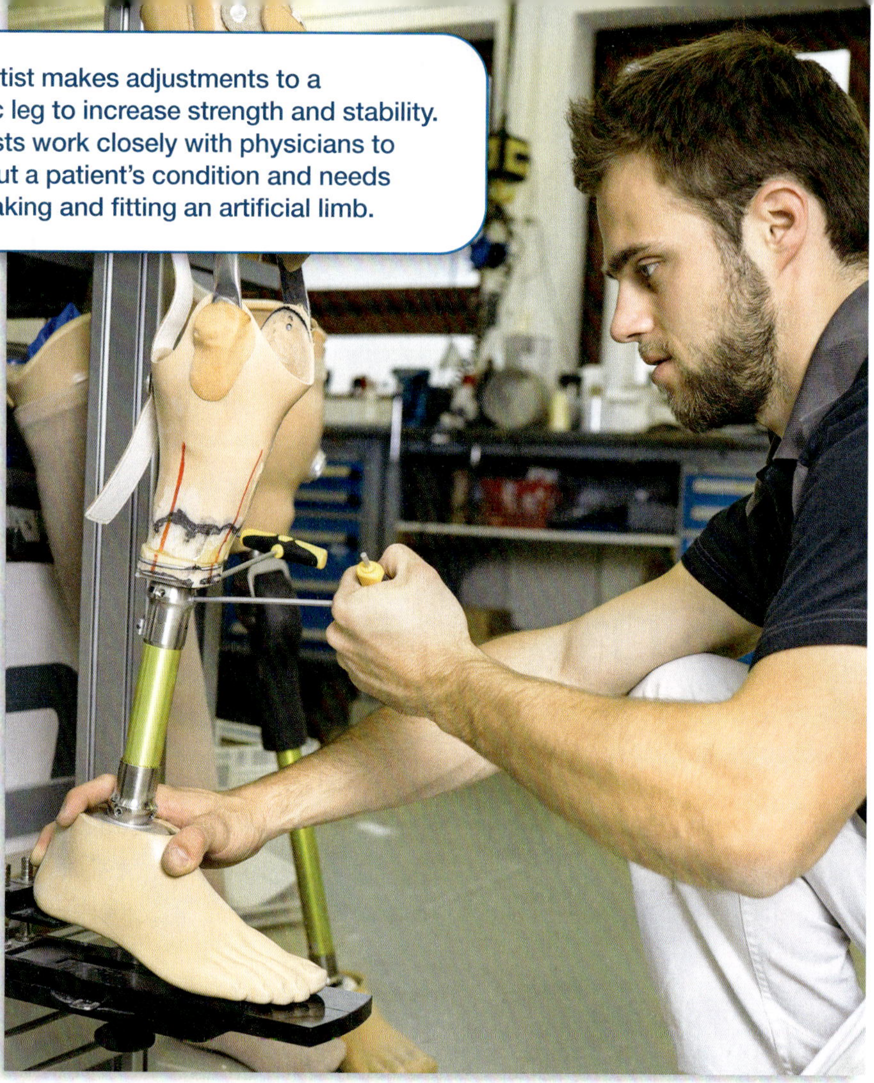

A prosthetist makes adjustments to a prosthetic leg to increase strength and stability. Prosthetists work closely with physicians to learn about a patient's condition and needs before making and fitting an artificial limb.

There are small staircases and ramps, parallel bars, uneven surfaces, and treadmills. Overhead harnesses allow patients to walk without putting their entire weight on the prosthesis. These tools allow the prosthetist to adjust and fine-tune prostheses to maximize functionality and eliminate discomfort. Prosthetist Jessica Smit describes the fine-tuning process for a patient with a below-the-knee prosthesis: "The patient required a few adjustments to the socket to get him fully comfortable, so I had to grind some of the carbon fiber away. This involves putting on a lab coat, arm sleeves, gloves, goggles and a respirator to protect myself from the itchy carbon fiber particles that I am grinding off the socket."[23]

Like most medical professionals, Smit deals with a lot of administrative tasks at the end of the day. She needs to obtain authorizations from health insurance companies, order prosthetic parts, update patient schedules, and prepare notes for her next day's appointments.

Education and Training

Prosthetists are medical professionals who need a master of science in orthotics and prosthetics. College programs are accredited by a professional organization such as the Commission on Accreditation of Allied Health Education Programs. High school students who hope to become prosthetists should take coursework in biology, chemistry, physics, psychology, algebra, and human anatomy.

Beyond the four years of undergraduate work, master's degree programs generally take two more years to complete. Courses cover topics including anatomy, neuroscience, biomechanics, materials science, diagnostic imaging techniques, diagnostic fitting, and kinesiology (the study of human movement). Students need to submit a thesis or research paper to graduate. After completing their degree program, students enter a twelve-month residency program to work with patients under the supervision of licensed prosthetists. This experience provides hands-on clinical experience in which residents assess patients, implement treatment plans, document patient progress, and communicate with patients and caregivers,

Prosthetists are required to obtain a license to practice in fifteen states. While certification is not required in most states, students often chose to attain accreditation to prove their proficiency and improve their job prospects. To become certified, students who have completed their master's program can take a multiple-choice, online exam provided by the American Board for Certification in Orthotics, Prosthetics & Pedorthics.

Skills and Personality

Losing a limb is a traumatic, life-altering experience for most people. Prosthetists need excellent interpersonal skills, what is referred to in medicine as a good bedside manner. Prosthetist/orthotist Todd Clay writes that his work "is not just about the mastery of science and technology but also about the art of understanding and compassion."[24] Clay says he listens closely to the concerns and goals of his patients and sometimes provides positive psychological support to help them overcome setbacks.

Prosthetists need good technical and computer skills to design and fabricate prostheses. The work is detail oriented; prosthetists are required to take exact measurements of body parts and need to be very precise when fine-tuning appliances.

There are physical aspects to the job that require prosthetists to be in good shape. The work involves bending, crouching, and sometimes physically supporting patients. Prosthetists are required to have good dexterity to fabricate, adapt, and adjust prostheses, which may have many mechanical parts.

Workplace Settings

Most prosthetists work full time in clinics, hospitals, and laboratories. They work with tools like electric drills and sanders that release harmful materials like carbon fiber or metal filings. Prosthetists might also be exposed to plastics and various toxic chemicals used in the fabrication process. Some face psychological problems when working with patients who have recently experienced trauma, but Stevens says the job provides personal satisfaction. "It's a very inspiring [way] to spend the day," he writes. "Patients come in with overwhelming challenges, and we get to help overcome them."[25]

Employers and Pay

Some prosthetists work for health care companies, hospitals, and medical equipment manufacturing companies. The Bureau

Building Trust by Listening

"Every patient has a story that significantly impacts their care and rehabilitation journey. When someone comes in for an evaluation, I make it a point to ask about their life. Understanding their experiences, hobbies, and personal challenges allows us to develop a customized plan that aligns with their goals and helps them achieve the best possible outcomes. Knowing their story is key to providing compassionate and effective care. This approach not only honors the individual behind the patient but also fosters a deeper connection and trust, which is essential for successful treatment."

—Todd Clay, prosthetist/orthotist

Todd Clay, "Embracing the Journey: My Path to Becoming a Prosthetist/Orthotist," Hanger Clinic, November 5, 2024. https://hangerclinic.com.

of Labor Statistics (BLS) says the median annual pay for prosthetists and orthotists was $78,310 in 2024. Those who worked for medical equipment manufacturers earned $83,220, while those who worked for clinics earned $74,600. Prosthetists in the upper 10 percent of wage earners brought in more than $118,730.

What Is the Future Outlook for Prosthetists?

There is a high demand for prosthetists. The BLS predicts employment for prosthetists and orthotists to grow by 15 percent through 2033, much faster than the average growth rate of 4 percent for all occupations. These figures are based on the fact that the general population is aging. The increase of age- and diet-related health issues like diabetes is expected to create a growing number of patients who will require the skills of prosthetists.

Find Out More

American Academy of Orthotists and Prosthetists

www.oandp.org

This organization promotes education, research, collaboration, and advocacy for what it refers to as the O&P profession. The academy offers publications, podcasts, conferences, and certification exams for prosthetists.

American Board for Certification in Orthotics, Prosthetics & Pedorthics (ABCOP)

www.abcop.org

The ABCOP is a credentialing organization for prosthetists, orthotists, and pedorthics (foot and ankle specialists). Its website offers career resources, news and events, and comprehensive information about the certification process.

National Commission on Orthotic and Prosthetic Education (NCOPE)

https://ncope.org

NCOPE is an educational resource that develops standards for accredited orthotics and prosthetics programs. Its website provides a Future Student FAQ section, professional academic programs, certifications, and resident training opportunities.

Aircraft Maintenance Technician

What Does an Aircraft Maintenance Technician Do?

A Boeing 747 is one of the most complicated machines ever built. It has over a million parts that make up its jet engines, control surfaces, landing gear, lift devices, flight instruments, control panels, electronic and hydraulic systems, and other components. Smaller airplanes and helicopters are less complex. But all aircraft, from small single-engine Cessna airplanes to the massive, US military King Stallion helicopters, need to be regularly serviced and repaired. Those who perform this work are called aircraft maintenance technicians (AMTs). Without their knowledge and skills, aircraft would not fly.

Aircraft maintenance technicians are also known as aviation and avionics equipment mechanics. AMTs service, repair, and overhaul vital components and make sure that every part of an aircraft is operating efficiently and safely. To protect against mechanical failure, those who work as AMTs use hand tools and power tools to replace defective parts on everything from jet engines to broken seats in a passenger compartment. They might also perform major

At a Glance

Number of Jobs
163,300 in 2023

Pay
$79,140 in 2024

Educational Requirements
Certificate from an FAA-approved aviation maintenance technical school

Personal Qualities
Mechanical aptitude, excellent observational and communication skills, good physical condition

Working Conditions
Full time outdoors in all types of weather

Future Job Outlook
Growth of 5 percent through 2033

overhauls or upgrades on flight systems in order to meet updated regulations from the Federal Aviation Administration (FAA), which oversees all aspects of American civil aviation. Aircraft maintenance technician Ehab Zaki describes his job at American Airlines: "We work on planes from the nose to the tail. Every time a plane lands, it needs to be serviced. It's an exciting job with a new set of challenges to solve every day."[26]

There are a number of specializations in the field of aviation maintenance. Some specialize in powerplants and airframes. Powerplants range from huge jet engines mounted on an aircraft's wings to piston-powered engines with propellers that can be installed either on the wings or in the nose. An airframe is the body of an aircraft and includes elements such as the fuselage, wings, tail assembly, and undercarriage. Those who specialize in avionics focus on electronic components that control flight, engine functions, navigation, communications, weather radar systems, and autopilots.

A Typical Workday

Aircraft maintenance technicians work in teams. The day begins with briefings, at which they receive assignments, review maintenance logs, and conduct equipment checks to confirm all required tools and parts are available. Routine inspections are a big part of the job. AMTs visually inspect tires, landing gear, hydraulic systems, engines, and wing mechanisms for leaks, wear, and malfunctioning components. Electrical systems are checked using electronic gauges called multimeters.

When inspections are completed, AMTs make necessary repairs. They might have to replace tires or worn-out brake pads, install new hydraulic hoses, or replace chips in computer systems. After repairs are made, AMTs troubleshoot the components to make sure they are operating properly. Every repair, no matter how small, must be recorded in an aircraft's maintenance log.

Move on from Mistakes

"At first you're going to be so nervous because you don't want to [mess] up. . . . You're going to make a mistake. What's important is you learn from it and move forward. Now I work nights from 9 pm to 7:30 am at [ORD, O'Hare International Airport in Chicago]. I love it! Even when it's –30 degree wind-chill in ORD, the work is still manageable and enjoyable. I work till it's all done then I can go to the break room and sleep, play on my laptop or talk with coworkers. Sometimes you work ALL night but more often than not you don't."

—Eicosapen, aircraft mechanic

Quoted in Reddit, "What Is It Like Being an Aircraft Mechanic?," 2025. www.reddit.com.

Preventative maintenance is another important aspect of an AMTs job. Moving parts are lubricated, bolts are tightened, fluid levels are checked, and filters and spark plugs are replaced on a regular schedule. Whatever procedures an AMT performs, the work must be done according to strict FAA guidelines. Technical writer Jennifer Caron explains, "[The AMT's] work is detailed, regulated, and stringent. They use a laptop as much as they use a wrench. Even routine tasks are step-by-step, and to the letter with secondary systems and redundancies in place, so there's no room for cutting corners or making mistakes. . . . These skills can take years of service, training, and education to develop and master."[27]

Education and Training

Many AMTs begin their rigorous training in the US Air Force or other branches of the armed forces working on military aircraft. Those who have not served in the military learn the trade at FAA-approved aviation maintenance technician schools. Caron says, "AMTs are not just your average run-of-the-mill mechanics. They

Aircraft maintenance technicians work on large airliners, small private planes, and helicopters. Their job is to service, repair, and overhaul vital aircraft components to make sure that every part of an aircraft is operating efficiently and safely.

are held to the highest standard of safety. AMTs start with a rigorous FAA training and certification process, and they don't stop learning until they retire."[28] Prospective AMTs can make their high school years count by taking classes in electronics, math, and computers. Auto shop classes teach valuable skills, including how engines and hydraulic and electronic systems function. While cars are mechanically different from airplanes, some skills can be transferred to AMT work.

A high school diploma is required to attend an FAA-approved program at an aviation maintenance technical school. These schools provide certificates of completion that allow students to take FAA exams relevant to their field. There are about 190 FAA-approved schools in the United States. By law, students who graduate from one of these schools must have completed nineteen hundred class hours, generally over the course of two years. Depending on their major (aviation technology, avionics, aviation maintenance), students complete courses in math, physics, chemistry, computer science, and mechanical drawing.

FAA certification is not required to become an AMT. However, most students seek accreditation because it improves their employment prospects and earning potential. Additionally, those without credentials can only work under supervision of certified mechanics. The FAA offers two types of certification: an airframe mechanic (A) is certified for body work, while a powerplant mechanic (P) works on engines. Most employers prefer those who have both certifications; they are called A&P mechanics. To obtain certification, technicians must be at least eighteen years old and US citizens who can read, write, and speak English. An applicant must have at least eighteen months of work experience to qualify for either an A or a P certification or thirty months of work to qualify for an A&P certification. Work requirements can be met by successfully completing courses at an aviation maintenance technical school. To obtain certification, applicants must pass a number of oral, written, and practical exams within a period of two years.

Avionics techs usually possess an airframe certification but can obtain other types of credentials. The National Center for Aerospace & Transportation Technologies issues an aircraft electronics technician certification. Avionics techs who work on communications equipment might need a radiotelephone operator certification issued by the Federal Communications Commission.

Skills and Personality

Employers prefer AMTs who are self-motivated, are hardworking, and exhibit a high degree of mechanical aptitude. AMTs spend their days multitasking as they diagnose and solve complex problems. AMTs rely on sharp eyesight to see the smallest imperfections in complex systems. They often listen for unusual engine noises that indicate problems. Aviation safety inspector Guy Minor, who began working on airplanes in high school, says, "Your

A Wide Variety of Opportunities

"As an aviation maintenance technician for an airline you'll receive great pay, good [paid time off] and retirement benefits, and the ability to switch to other bases with enough seniority. There are a variety of opportunities in different sectors like the airlines, private aviation, and cargo carriers. Working in aviation maintenance offers the chance to perform various tasks including routine maintenance, repair work, inspections, and even retrofitting. . . . Whether you're working on cutting-edge technology for private jets or ensuring military aircraft are ready for missions, there's a wide range of paths you can take in this field."

—Jon Dillenberg, airframe and powerplant technician

Jon Dillenberg, "The Pros and Cons of Being an Aircraft Mechanic," Thrust Institute of Maintenance, December 23, 2024. www.thrustinstitute.com.

senses tell you a lot about the airplane. You can smell things when they're hot or if an engine is worn out or low in oil, it has a certain smell."[29] AMTs need strong reading and writing skills. They have to read and understand a whole array of FAA regulations. And when they do repair or maintenance work on aircraft, the FAA requires them to write detailed reports documenting all work performed.

The job of an AMT is physically demanding. During the course of a day, AMTs will spend hours standing on concrete, crouching, reaching, walking up and down jet bridge stairs, and performing repairs while kneeling or even lying down. They twist their bodies to awkward positions and lift tires and mechanical parts that can weigh more than 50 pounds (22.7 kg).

Workplace Settings

Aircraft maintenance technicians work full time. Airplanes fly around the clock, and they need maintenance and repair services days, nights, weekends, and holidays. AMTs at major airlines and freight companies can expect to put in a lot of overtime, working as much as fifty-five to sixty hours a week.

Aircraft maintenance technicians are exposed to all types of weather. They work in huge, open airplane hangars or on airport aprons, outdoor areas where aircraft are parked. In the summer AMTs in Texas or Arizona might be performing their duties when temperatures rise to over 110°F (43°C). Those in Wisconsin work in snow and ice when temperatures plunge below freezing in the winter. The job can be dangerous for other reasons. AMTs work around moving propellers and incredibly loud jet engines. They are exposed to a wide range of hazardous oils, fuels, and chemicals like toluene, which is used for cleaning.

Employers and Pay

Aircraft maintenance technicians work for major airlines like Delta Air Lines, Southwest Airlines, and American Airlines. They are also employed by freight companies that transport mail, packages, and merchandise. Some work in what is called general aviation, maintaining propeller aircraft and helicopters that are owned by businesses, transportation companies, local television stations, and hobby pilots.

The Bureau of Labor Statistics (BLS) classifies aircraft maintenance technicians as aircraft and avionics equipment mechanics and technicians. The median annual wage for aircraft maintenance technician was $79,140 in 2024. Those who worked for major airlines earned $95,320 annually. Avionics technicians at major airlines earned the highest wages, $99,150 annually. AMTs employed by the federal government were paid less, earning an average salary of $72,920.

What Is the Future Outlook for Aircraft Maintenance Technicians?

The BLS says employment for all aircraft and avionics equipment mechanics and technicians is expected to grow by 5 percent through 2033, slightly higher than the 4 percent average growth rate for all professions. The demand for avionics technicians is expected to increase by 8 percent through 2033. With airlines as busy as ever, and cargo companies delivering consumer goods around the clock, those who specialize in servicing and repairing aircraft will be in demand.

Find Out More

Aircraft Electronics Association (AEA)
https://aea.net
The AEA represents numerous government-certified repair facilities and equipment manufacturers along with avionics engineers and educational institutions. The association offers training courses, scholarships, and publications of interest to students and avionics workers.

Aviation Institute of Maintenance (AIM)
https://aviationmaintenance.edu
The AIM is an educational institution that provides instruction in FAA-approved courses. Its website describes details concerning numerous courses that allow students to pursue careers as avionics technicians, aviation maintenance technicians, and helicopter mechanics.

Federal Aviation Administration (FAA)
www.faa.gov/mechanics/become
The FAA regulates all airlines in the United States. The administration's web page "Become an Aviation Mechanic" explains career and wage information and describes certification requirements to become an A&P mechanic.

Veterinarian

What Does a Veterinarian Do?

Melanie Wood was walking with her mom when they discovered a large black dog trapped in a drainage pipe holding several feet of water. The dog could not stop swimming or it would drown. Wood's mom jumped down into the water and managed to save the dog. Wood, who was ten years old at the time, ran to get her wagon and pulled the wet, exhausted, black lab mix home. After the dog recovered, it was reunited with its family. Wood says the event had a profound impact on her. She recalls, "The feeling I got from what little part I played in that rescue and reunion inspired me to continue to help animals for the rest of my life. Helping animals growing up was the foundation for the inspiration to pursue the field of veterinary medicine."[30] Like most in her profession, Wood loves animals and enjoys helping and healing them. And as a veterinarian, says she has rescued dozens of stray dogs, cats, birds, turtles, and even chipmunks.

At a Glance

Number of Jobs
86,400 in 2024

Pay
$125,510 in 2024

Educational Requirements
Doctoral degree

Personal Qualities
Compassionate, emotionally strong, good communication skills, manual dexterity, problem-solving skills

Working Conditions
In offices, animal clinics and hospitals, farms, zoos, and a variety of research facilities

Future Job Outlook
Growth of 19 percent through 2033

A veterinarian is formally referred to as a doctor of veterinary medicine (DVM). And rescuing animals is only one part of a DVM's job. Veterinarians spend their days examining animals, running medical tests, and diagnosing health problems. They treat and dress wounds, address dental problems, set fractured bones, perform surgery, prescribe medications, and vaccinate animals from diseases. Veterinarians use medical tools like syringes, scalpels, and X-ray and ultrasound machines. When animals are suffering from terminal diseases and other uncurable problems, veterinarians provide end-of-life care and humanely euthanize animals. Most veterinarians will say this task, which often includes counseling grieving pet owners, is the most difficult part of the job.

Veterinarians most often practice as specialists. Those who work as companion animal, or small animal, veterinarians treat pets including dogs, cats, rabbits, ferrets, and birds. They consult with owners about a pet's diets, behavior problems, and preventative health care. Like physicians who treat people, some vets work in specialty medicine such as ophthalmology (eyes), cardiology (heart), internal medicine, dermatology (skin), and oncology (cancer).

Food animal veterinarians, also called large animal vets, work with livestock, including pigs, cattle, and sheep, that are raised to be eaten. Those referred to as equine veterinarians treat large animals including horses, mules, donkeys, and llamas. Like small animal vets, these veterinarians treat wounds, set fractures, perform surgery, and vaccinate against diseases.

Food-safety and inspection veterinarians inspect and test livestock for diseases like salmonella that might be transmitted between animals and humans. These vets ensure that animal welfare laws are enforced so that animals are treated as humanely as possible.

A Typical Workday

The daily tasks performed by a veterinarian depends on their practice and the needs of their animal patients. Those who work with companion animals try to divide their days into two parts. Half the day is spent in prebooked surgical appointments that

Helping Pets and Families

"Being an urgent care and emergency vet . . . is both an incredible privilege and a constant challenge. Every day, pet parents trust me with their beloved companions in their most vulnerable moments. The human–animal bond is powerful, making it heartbreaking to see pets in pain. Knowing that I can be there for families during their most difficult times, providing the urgent care and compassion they need, gives me strength and purpose. Providing that support means everything to me. It's what keeps me going and reminds me daily of the profound impact we can have on the lives of both pets and their people."

—K.C. Van Fleet, emergency and urgent care veterinarian

K.C. Van Fleet, "A Day in the Life of an Emergency and Urgent Care Veterinarian," Omnivet, August 18, 2025. https://omnivet.org.

might include spaying or neutering, removing lesions and other masses, or performing specialized procedures such as dentistry, cancer surgery, or joint replacement. Depending on the type of surgery, operations might last forty-five minutes to several hours.

The second half of a companion animal veterinarian's day is used to conduct physical exams, which include checking an animal's eyes, mouth, ears, legs, tail, belly, rear end, and reproductive organs. Time is often set aside for emergency appointments when animals have been hit by cars, been in fights, or sustained nonurgent injuries.

Veterinarians consult with pet owners in person, on the phone, by text, or through telemedicine calls. Like most professions, veterinarians deal with paperwork. They maintain detailed medical histories for each pet that include treatments, prescribed medicines, and surgical records. Veterinary consultant Kimberly Simmons remembers her days as a DVM: "Toward the end of the day, I would help the staff give treatments to those pets that are in the hospital, and [clean] up to get ready for the next day! It seems like a lot, but it was quite enjoyable, especially seeing the animals who were sick get better, and being able to play and meet all of the pets coming in to see me!"[31] Most clinics employ veterinary technicians who help with paperwork, provide intake examinations, weigh animals, take blood samples, and give shots.

Pet care technician Krista Vollbrecht treats horses. Describing her average workday, she says, "Equine veterinarians typically travel to their clients. . . . The number of clients they see a day as well as the types of procedures they do can vary from day to day. One day, you might see one client with 20 horses that all need vaccines and routine dental work, and the next day you might see 4 clients with 2 horses each that need vaccines, dental work, stitches, etc."[32]

Education and Training

Every veterinarian has a DVM degree from an accredited college. Applicants to veterinary medicine programs need a bachelor's degree in a related field such as biology. Admission to veterinary medicine programs is very competitive. Schools favor applicants who have previously completed courses in animal science, microbiology, physics, anatomy, and chemistry. Those who wish to stay ahead of the competition can gain experience in high school by taking the related courses, volunteering at an animal shelter, or working at a stable or on a farm.

A DVM program usually takes four years to complete. Courses cover subjects that include animal physiology, immunology, pathology, pharmacology, and surgical techniques. Students study individual animal species, body systems, and medical procedures. Courses are conducted in classrooms and laboratories, and all students are required to work in clinical rotations, seeing animal patients under the supervision of experienced DVM mentors.

Like all doctors, veterinarians perform exams, run medical tests, and diagnose and treat health problems. But instead of working with human patients, they work with animals. The tools of their trade include stethoscopes, syringes, scalpels, and X-ray and ultrasound machines.

DVMs who want to pursue specialty areas often work one year as interns or two to three years as clinical residents. Every state has licensing requirements for veterinarians, and most require DVMs to pass the North American Veterinary Licensing Examination or similar exam.

Skills and Personality

Compassion is the number one job requirement for most veterinarians, especially those who work with sick pets and worried owners on a daily basis. People love their pets, and veterinarians need to be sensitive and gentle when they handle animals.

Good communication skills are a must for veterinarians, who need to describe details of a pet's diagnosis in empathetic terms

Treating Animals at a Zoo

"Unlike other realms of veterinary medicine, zoological medicine entails more logistical planning, as many species are potentially dangerous to work with and ensuring human and animal safety is imperative. . . . For each immobilization, we had a set drill. The veterinary technicians and students would load up the van with crates of medical supplies, drugs, oxygen, anesthetic equipment, and more while the veterinarian prepared their anesthetic protocol and darts. Essentially, we had a mobile hospital ready to tend to any animal anywhere in the zoo. Rain or shine, pleasant or frigid weather, the veterinary team was always ready to spring into action."

—Alexander Levitskiy, veterinary student at New York City's Bronx Zoo

Alexander Levitskiy, "'The Zoo' Through the Eyes of a Veterinary Student," Cornell K. Lisa Yang Center for Wildlife Health, June 11, 2024. https://wildlife.cornell.edu.

while also outlining treatments or—in worst-case scenarios—euthanasia. As DVM Katie J. Reese puts it, "Just remember that you don't need to internalize somebody else's emotions to be compassionate. Just being a witness and conveying to your client that they are not alone is an act of compassion."[33]

Veterinarians also need to be emotionally strong themselves when working with animals that have been severely injured, have been abandoned, or cannot be saved. DVM Julie Cappel counsels veterinarians with these words: "Emotionally strong people realize that life is both positive and negative. They understand that there are negative things in life that are beyond their control. They do not feel sorry for themselves when bad things happen because they know that it is part of the deal."[34]

While the work can sometimes be emotional, veterinarians must remain focused and analytical. They need strong problem-solving skills when diagnosing animals and must make quick decisions when providing treatment. In addition to these mental abilities, veterinarians also rely on manual dexterity, especially when performing surgery.

Workplace Settings

Workplace settings for veterinarians vary according to their specialty. Those who treat companion animals in clinics usually work forty hours a week with overtime when emergencies arise. Some vets work at emergency clinics, where pets with critical conditions can be treated at any time of the day. Veterinarians in these places typically work in shifts, from 8:00 a.m. to 4:00 p.m., 4:00 p.m. to midnight, or midnight to 8:00 a.m.

Large animal vets often keep their gear and medicines in a truck, enabling them to provide on-site care at barns, corrals, and pastures. Other large animal vets are employed by zoos or wildlife rescue facilities and work as part of a caretaking team. Specialists in large animal veterinary medicine usually work forty hours a week but must be available nights, weekends, and holidays for emergencies. Food-safety and inspection veterinarians also work forty hours a week with overtime in feedlots, slaughterhouses, and food processing plants. They also work in labs where they test livestock for diseases.

Employers and Pay

Large and small animal veterinarians often run their own clinics or work as part of a team in a shared practice. Food-safety and inspection veterinarians are usually employed by state or federal government agencies or by food producers. The Bureau of Labor Statistics (BLS) says the median salary for all veterinarians was $125,510 in 2024. Those who worked for government agencies earned an average of $111,420.

What Is the Future Outlook for Veterinarians?

The BLS predicts the demand for veterinarians will grow by 19 percent through 2033. This is much faster than the average growth rate of 4 percent for all occupations. Consumers are spending more on their pets every year, and veterinary medicine is advancing with new treatments for cancer, kidney problems, and other ailments. These factors are driving the strong employment statistics for DVMs.

Find Out More

American Association of Veterinary Medical Colleges (AAVMC)

www.aavmc.org

The AAVMC is focused on educational resources for veterinary students. Its website offers programs and initiatives that cover accreditation, animal welfare instruction, and professional development.

American Veterinary Medical Association (AVMA)

www.avma.org

The AVMA is a leading organization for prospective veterinarians and veterinary professionals. The association's website provides information about accredited veterinary colleges, internships, educational resources, and certification services.

International Council for Veterinary Assessment (ICVA)

www.icva.net

The ICVA administers the North American Veterinary Licensing Examination. Visitors to the ICVA website can find study guides for the exam and information about veterinary licensing agencies in every US state and Canadian province.

Source Notes

Introduction: Skilled Workers in Demand

1. Quoted in Farah Stockman, "Why Factories Are Having Trouble Filling Nearly 400,00 Jobs," *New York Times*, June 23, 2025. www.nytimes.com.
2. Quoted in Resume Builder, "4 in 10 Gen Z College Grads Are Turning to Blue-Collar Work for Job Security," May 20, 2025. www.resumebuilder.com.
3. Quoted in Resume Builder, "4 in 10 Gen Z College Grads Are Turning to Blue-Collar Work for Job Security."
4. Gina Balistreri, "New Report from Thumbtack Examines Forces Behind Skilled Trade Labor Shortage, Offering Optimistic Outlook for the Future," Thumbtack, 2025. https://press.thumbtack.com.
5. Quoted in Balistreri, "New Report from Thumbtack Examines Forces Behind Skilled Trade Labor Shortage, Offering Optimistic Outlook for the Future."

Tattoo Artist

6. Quoted in Mike Bayer, "Inked: Nikko Hurtado, Secrets from a Celebrity Tattoo Artist!," Coach Mike, March 10, 2020. https://coachmikebayer.com.
7. Quoted in Lilianna Maria Percy Ruiz, "Thinking of Getting Inked? Start with a Tiny Tattoo," NPR, February 15, 2024. www.npr.org.
8. Veronique Wiebe, "Meet Veronique Wiebe," Canvas Rebel, May 16, 2024. https://canvasrebel.com.
9. Quoted in Bayer, "Inked."

Electrician

10. Carl Murawski, "20-Year Career as an Electrician—Would I Do It Again?," Carl Murawski, September 24, 2024. https://carlmurawski.com.

11. Murawski, "20-Year Career as an Electrician—Would I Do It Again?"
12. Quoted in Quora, "How Many Times Does an Electrician Get Shocked over a 30 Year Career?," 2022. www.quora.com.
13. Quoted in Reddit, "What Is Day to Day Like as an Electrician?," 2024. www.reddit.com.

Archaeologist

14. Sarah W. Neusius, "How I Became an Archaeologist," Carnegie Museum of Natural History, 2025. https://carnegiemnh.org.
15. Andrea M. Berlin, "A Career in Archaeology," Archaeological Institute of America, 2025. www.archaeological.org.
16. Sam Tabner, "A Day in the Life of an Archaeologist," Reading Museum, July 15, 2020. www.readingmuseum.org.uk.
17. Berlin, "A Career in Archaeology."
18. Smiti, "About," Habits of a Traveling Archeologist, 2023. https://habitsofatravellingarchaeologist.com.
19. Mara Kaktins, "Archaeology Is Not for the Faint of Heart—But We Love It Anyway," *Lives & Legacies* (blog), November 15, 2024. https://livesandlegaciesblog.org.

Prosthetist

20. Quoted in Emily H. Bratcher, "Orthotist and Prosthetist Overview," *U.S. News & World Report*, 2025. https://money.usnews.com.
21. Quoted in Emily H. Bratcher, "Orthotist and Prosthetist Reviews and Advice," *U.S. News & World Report*, 2025. https://money.usnews.com.
22. Annie Crain, "A Day in the Life of Annie Crain Resident Prosthetist/Orthotist," *The Exponential Factor* (blog), Louisiana Tech University Department of Kinesiology, October 12, 2022. https://kinesiologyexponentialfactor.blog.
23. Jessica Smit, "A Day in the Life: Jessica Smit, Certified Prosthetist Orthotist," Shirley Ryan AbilityLab, April 23, 2025. www.sralab.org.

24. Todd Clay, "Embracing the Journey: My Path to Becoming a Prosthetist/Orthotist," Hanger Clinic, November 5, 2024. https://hangerclinic.com.
25. Quoted in Bratcher, "Orthotist and Prosthetist Reviews and Advice."

Aircraft Maintenance Technician

26. Quoted in Vaughn College, "Aviation Maintenance Graduate Ehab Zaki '21 Proves It's Never Too Late to Pursue Your Dream Career," May 31, 2022. www.vaughn.edu.
27. Jennifer Caron, "Not Just Your Average Mechanic," *FAA Safety Briefing*, March 4, 2022. https://medium.com.
28. Caron, "Not Just Your Average Mechanic."
29. Quoted in Caron, "Not Just Your Average Mechanic."

Veterinarian

30. Melanie Wood, "What Inspired Me to Become a Veterinarian," Main Street Animal Hospital, 2025. https://mainstreet-animalhospital.com.
31. Kimberly Simmons, "What Are Some Daily Tasks for Veterinarians?," CareerVillage.org, 2025. www.careervillage.org.
32. Krista Vollbrecht, "What Are Some Daily Tasks for Veterinarians?," CareerVillage.org, 2025. www.careervillage.org.
33. Quoted in Malinda Larkin, "Showing Compassion Benefits Practitioner, Client Alike," AVMA, January 6, 2023. www.avma.org.
34. Julie Cappel, "Using Your Emotional Strength," Mission Veterinary Partners, 2025. https://missionvetpartners.com.

Interview with an Archaeologist

Andrea M. Berlin is an archaeologist and professor who began her teaching career in 1997. She is currently the James R. Wiseman Chair in Classical Archaeology and a professor of archaeology and religion at Boston University. This interview was conducted by email.

Q: Why did you decide to become an archaeologist?

A: I went on a dig! When I was 17 years old, I worked on a two-week excavation at the ancient city of Be'er Sheva in Israel. We slept in tents and woke up at 4:30 every morning to get started. Every other person on the trip hated it, but to me it was like a history book come to life in front of my eyes. When I got down in a trench and cleared away the dirt, I was standing in the 8th century BCE, holding a pot that no one had seen for 3,000 years. I could imagine another young girl's hands picking it up. I felt like a time traveler.

I heard my supervisor speaking about getting classes ready for the fall semester, and I said to him, "You mean somebody *pays* you to do this?" He laughed and said yes. And I said to myself, that's it. This is what I'm going to do.

Q: Can you describe your typical workday (or night)?

A: I work in lands around the Mediterranean, where it is hot in the summer. On a typical workday, we're in the field by 5:30 a.m., putting in a full day's work by noon. Then we come in from the field, eat lunch, maybe shower and rest for an hour or so. By mid-afternoon, we are back at it with paperwork. We record artifacts that were found that day, draw plans, and so on. This usually lasts until dinner time and sometimes continues after dinner, too. Finally, it's lights out, and [we get] a good night's sleep so that we can get up early again the next day.

Excavations are intense, and sometimes a little dangerous. Potential hazards include blisters, injury from tools or large rocks, or even falling into one of the deep holes created on the site. That said, in my almost 50 years of excavating, I only broke one bone . . . while moving rocks.

Q: What do you like most about your job?

A: I like pretty much everything about it! I think I've never had a day when I wasn't delighted to be an archaeologist. I love being outside, working with other people, and discovering new things. I love doing research on places and objects I discover because I am super curious. I enjoy the challenge of writing in such a way that my ideas come across; I want others to benefit from my discoveries and get excited about them. The last part of my job, teaching at a university, is also very satisfying. I get to introduce students to this amazing subject, nurture their excitement, and widen their worldview.

I think the best thing about being an archaeologist is that it has given me a personal connection with the past and with hundreds of anonymous—but real—people. It is magical, humbling, mysterious, and thrilling. It makes the past real and alive, and it reminds me that it was filled with regular people going about their daily lives, just like today.

Q: What do you like least about your job?

A: Recording, studying, and writing; I always have more to do than time to do it. This can be stressful, like having too much homework. Maybe the biggest drawback is the job doesn't pay as well as many careers, especially considering how much schooling you need. Also, you can end up devoting much or all of your time to it. I know many archaeologists who never married or had children, and who truly gave themselves over to their career (but they were very happy).

Q: What personal qualities do you find most valuable for this type of work?

A: The big three: curiosity, patience, and imagination. Also critical: love of learning (this never ends) and the ability to be part of a team, working together. Plus stamina. Because it's not just an expression: when you go on a dig, you should expect to *dig*. Archaeologists should be in good physical condition and be able to move and bend easily. You must not mind getting dirty and hot—and you should enjoy being outside.

Archaeology requires a natural attention to detail, to being careful and attentive. We remove dirt carefully so that we can tell how things came to be situated as they were; we record it carefully so that we can reconstruct what happened in the past.

Q: What advice do you have for students who might be interested in a career as an archaeologist?

A: Go on a dig! If you are interested in archaeology as a career, the best thing that you can do is find out about excavations where you live. Good sources of information are state highway and natural resource departments, local historical societies, and local colleges. Almost every state has a state archaeologist; that person can let you know if there are local digs that you can volunteer for. Another resource is local contract archaeology firms, who carry out surveys and excavations on federal, state, or city lands. Almost any project will happily accept volunteer workers, and high-school-age students are definitely old enough. (I once directed a crew of 10- to 12-year-olds for two weeks, and they were terrific!)

Excavations also need people with special skills. These include technical drawing, photography, mapping and surveying, and various computer applications, especially GIS [geographic information system] and database management. If you know how to do one or more of these, you can be very useful on an excavation.

Other Jobs If You Like Working with Your Hands

Animator
Beekeeper
Butcher
Cake decorator
Carpenter
Chef
Comic book artist
Craft artist
Diesel service technician
Drafter
Drywall installer
Farmer
Fashion designer
Fine artist
Fishing and hunting guide
Floral designer
Glazier
Hairstylist
Ironworker
Jewelry designer
Landscape designer
Machinist
Medical illustrator
Musician
Plumber
Rancher
Robotics engineer
Screen printer
Surveyor
Tailor
Weaver
Welder

Editor's note: The online *Occupational Outlook Handbook* of the US Department of Labor's Bureau of Labor Statistics is an excellent source of information on jobs in hundreds of career fields, including many of those listed here. The *Occupational Outlook Handbook* may be accessed online at www.bls.gov/ooh.

Index

Picture Credits

Cover: LP Design/Shutterstock

10: Goami/Shutterstock
19: Tong_stocker/Shutterstock
26: AntonChalakov/iStockphoto
34: Belushi/Shutterstock
42: EXTREME-PHOTOGRAPHER/iStockphoto
51: SeventyFour/Shutterstock

About the Author

Stuart A. Kallen is the author of more than four hundred nonfiction books for children and young adults. He has written on topics ranging from the theory of relativity to making a career in the music industry. In 2018 Kallen won a Green Earth Book Award from the Nature Generation environmental organization. He has also written award-winning children's videos and TV scripts. In his spare time, he is a singer, songwriter, and guitarist in San Diego.